INTO THE DARKNESS...
Guided By His Light

by

Robin Strine

Just Believe
Ron Strine

Bloomington, IN

authorHOUSE®

Milton Keynes, UK

2 Corinthians 4:18

AuthorHouse™
1663 Liberty Drive, Suite 200
Bloomington, IN 47403
www.authorhouse.com
Phone: 1-800-839-8640

AuthorHouse™ UK Ltd.
500 Avebury Boulevard
Central Milton Keynes, MK9 2BE
www.authorhouse.co.uk
Phone: 08001974150

First published by AuthorHouse   10/8/2007

ISBN: 978-1-4343-1384-3 (sc)

Printed in the United States of America
Bloomington, Indiana

This book is printed on acid-free paper.

2 Corinthians 4:18

Everyday, I thank my God for my life, my son's life, and for giving me the passion to bring hope and encouragement to others. To all, who through life's circumstances, have had to learn to live in a "new normal", I pray that you will find the joy that comes with knowing our amazing God .

November, 2005

As I made my way out of the car, the leaves were rustling under my feet. The path to the house was covered with bright, yellow, fall leaves that had fallen from the big oak tree that stands in front of my home. I have taken this path many times. I have nine steps up the curvy sidewalk to get to the two steps that lead to the front door. After finding the keyhole, I make my way into the house that I have called home for the past thirteen years. The home where my son has grown up. The home where we have had many happy memories, sad times and moments that will never be forgotten. I make my way to the kitchen with supper that has been prepared this week by one of our friends. Tommy will be home soon, but for now I will rest after a seemingly long day.

The house is quiet and still and I snuggle down in my blue, denim couch. I think about the past and how when you can't see God's plan, you have to trust in His Heart.

Remembering

FIFTEEN YEARS AGO, I COULDN'T see God's plan for my life. I was a 26 year old, healthy woman that just wanted to be happy and married. On August 19, 1989, I said "I do" to a man that I planned to spend the rest of my life with.

The wedding was a time of joy. It was just like a fairy tale with beautiful flowers, songs, and poems. There were even a few laughs as my sister-in-law forgot to slow down for a curve when we were on our way to the reception with my brothers' Samari jeep.

Christmas was at our house that year. It was our first Christmas as husband and wife. What an exciting time for us as we picked out our Christmas tree and planned for the holiday. New Years came and went and we were looking forward to our first Valentines Day together. We had a spaghetti dinner together and received a book from my mom titled "Where's Mom Now That I Need Her." Little did we know that just two days later our lives would be turned upside down.

A Life Changing Moment

ICE COVERED EVERYTHING THAT Friday morning, February 16, 1990. The whole town was hearing ice crackle. The schools were all cancelled, but I was on my way to work in my 1989 Cutlass Cierra only to become the victim of a freak accident. I was about to become the center of attention. In my mid-twenties, I was newly married, buying a house and a new car, was the manager of my brothers tanning business and my time was about to end. But I did not write the script, God did.

I drove carefully along Clinton Street toward the tanning salon, wary of the icy roads. I turned left onto Indiana Avenue. A tree branch less than a mile away began to crackle and moan as it shuddered in the morning wind. As I approached the tree, the thick branch—14 inches in diameter—hung ominously over the road. I hoped the car in front of me could stop on the icy road. The branch tore away from the tree as I, completely unaware of the danger ahead, wondered if my 9 o'clock appointment would even show. It was 8:48 a.m. The second my car drove under the icy branch, estimated at 7,000 pounds, it snapped at the base, fell 15 feet and slammed onto the roof of my car. The windows shattered as the tree branch crushed the roof of my car onto my skull. My whole world went black.

My car continued through the snow, between a house and a traffic light pole and through a busy street intersection while the light was red. It finally came to rest on a gas line at the back of the building where I worked. Pieces of the ice-covered limb lay scattered across the road between Fifth and Seventh Street.

My brother, Rod, just returning home from a trip to Denver, pulled into the parking lot and seeing my crumpled car, knew that I had to be dead.

A Mothers Love

Sitting at my desk, I made a call to Robin to warn her of the icy roads. I cautioned her to stay home that day if she could. After saying good-bye, I hung up the phone to start the day not knowing what lie ahead. A little while later when the phone rang, I thought it might be Sam, my co-worker, telling me he would be late as he also drove a school bus and schools were delayed that day. Unfortunately, it was a neighbor asking me if I had heard that Robin was in an accident. My heart stopped and I screamed. Wild thoughts raced through my mind because I knew how bad the ice was. She told me that Randy, Robin's oldest brother, was on his way to get me. I hung up the phone and went out to the lobby where several people were sitting. I was hysterically saying "I need to get to Auburn! I need to get to Auburn!" over and over again. As soon as Randy arrived, I could tell by his face that it was very bad. I kept asking him if she was alive but all he would reply was that she was on her way to the hospital.

When I walked in the door of the hospital, it was terrible. I could sense the graveness. Since I had worked in the hospital for eight years and had spent some of that time in the emergency room, I knew how serious the situation was. I found myself on the opposite side of tragedy. I was the one being taken care of instead of my taking care of others.

With everyone gathered around me, the doctor told us to wait a few minutes before we left the hospital because he did not want us to try to keep up with the ambulance. They were in a hurry to get Robin transferred to a bigger hospital in Fort Wayne. They did not want to lose a second.

The drive to the hospital seemed to take an eternity. When we arrived, the EMT's were just coming back out of the hospital. With tears in my eyes and holding my breath, I dared to ask; "Is she still alive?" and they answered "YES!" We knew that we had already received one miracle but the next 72 hours would be critical.

A Daily Journal
Kept by Robin's mother

February 16, 1990

"Robin"

What a special child of God—from the very second of your accident, He has held you in His arms.

This morning, on your way to the salon, a large (12-16" in diameter) tree limb fell on the top of your car crushing your head down—the Lord took over the wheel and guided the car across the intersection on a red light. An oncoming car got stopped, and a pedestrian got out of the way. Your car went up on the sidewalk, between light posts and a house—over rocks— and broke a main gas line into the back of a building. Jesus held you in His arms every minute and guided the car to slowly stop without crashing. You are a miracle—with the rescue crew, the good Samaritan, the EMT's, and the fire

7

department all working to get you out.

Your brother, Rod, cannot believe how he happened to come home a day early from Denver and pull in the salon ten minutes after the ambulance. He saw the car and knew you had to be dead. The police told him they were on the way to a local hospital. A long time friend was there and went on ahead to the hospital. Another friend went also and was even in the ER before you. Rod called Randy to go get me before I heard. I was hysterical when I saw tears in Randy's eyes—thinking they were not telling me everything. Someone called Susie before even Rod—she called Rick and he came to get her. She will tell you how everyone was in place.

The second I entered the hospital I could tell by everyone's faces and the way they were holding on to me that the situation was very critical. So many people were there.

You were rushed to Lutheran by EMS—lights and sirens. At Lutheran you were in the ER for quite a while because they had to order a special bed to keep you in and special padding so you would not move. They kept you sedated most of the night. Rod called your dad in Denver and informed him of the seriousness of the accident and advised him to fly home ASAP. My pastor came right away to be with all of us. Your dad was here by 10 p.m. There were so many people in the ICU lounge that night to try to keep our spirits up and give encouragement.

Saturday, February 17, 1990

Hi, Robin, I went home at 5 a.m. this morning to bathe and change clothes—your dad is asleep in the chair. Rick and Susie were here until about 1 a.m. So many people were here to see you and we have had phone calls galore. It seemed like 500 at least. You are still critical at this point. The doctor came out to the lounge and said you should have been paralyzed for life or normally this could have caused death. The spinal cord has to be fused back together. This day is kind of a blur. Randy, Rod, Rick and Susie are staying here most of the time. Your accident was in this morning's newspaper and several people saw it on T.V.

Sunday, February 18, 1990

You are still sedated most of the time. Every 3-4 hours you wake up and need a pain shot. Every church you can imagine is having prayer for you. There are prayer chains everywhere—everyone wants to help—just to do anything for all of us. So many more family and friends are here today. It has been 48 hours and each hour gives us a little more hope. Neighbors of mine were here trying to keep everyone's spirits up. They were even able to get people to laugh and relieve the stress for a little bit. We are still getting tons of phone calls and your brother, Rod, is being swamped at the Salon with people asking about you. You have so many friends around you. The whole town of Auburn has been touched. So many people think of you as their own daughter.

Monday, February 19, 1990

Your brother took your dad to Rent-A-Car today. When they came back, the doctor talked to us about your back and the repair it will need. He was so kind. He is the orthopedic specialist and will be doing your back surgery.

Tuesday, February 20, 1990

This was probably the worst day—you wanted water so desperately that you would do almost anything. You just couldn't understand why no one would let you have it. By late afternoon, you started getting delirious and by evening you were having hallucinations.

Your sister-in-law, Susie, came this afternoon and stayed in with you for awhile, that really helped. Your nephews cannot understand why they can't see you. They keep drawing you pictures. Nick told all about you at school for "show and tell." Susie said he took the picture from the paper to school with him and explained everything.

Wednesday, February 21, 1990

I finally talked to the doctor at 12:30 today. You were so great—first you asked for more water which he increased. You wanted to go home and he explained that you will have back surgery later next week. He said your spine is loose and if it is not repaired you would be in a wheelchair for the rest of your life. You asked if you could at least go home until the surgery. You were so quick and alert that he was amazed at your progress so far.

Your orthopedic doctor saw me in the hall and was telling me that he really has to have better x-rays and it would be the first of the week before you could be moved to do a CT scan—so I said please don't schedule your surgery on March 7th because of your brother Rick's surgery. He would be having a brain tumor removed. The doctor could not believe it about Rick and said that he would work with the other doctors to get things worked out. When the doctor saw you, you asked for your surgery tomorrow so you would be better before Rick's surgery. He said that you will know what is happening.

I was talking to a lady who works here and she asked me who was in the hospital. I said that my daughter was and told her about the accident. She said that you are certainly a miracle and that you were so lucky to be alive. The other nurses told her that your recovery is remarkable.

Thursday, February 22, 1990

Your best day yet! You had your bath and the nurse washed your hair as good as she could. The nurse even cleaned your nails while I fed your lunch to you (milk, Jell-O, and pudding.)

We got to see you more and you asked about the accident. We are all so happy that you are doing better—everyone is so encouraged.

Friday, February 23, 1990

You are not feeling so good today. You are having more pain, headaches mostly. We are just waiting for the doctor and you have been sleeping most of the day.

Praise the Lord—6:30 p.m. You are out of the ICU and were moved to the 2nd floor to a room by the window. Your brothers came in to see you and brought some pictures of the car. We all thought that it would be alright for you to see them.

Saturday, February 24, 1990

When I got to the hospital you said that your doctors had already been here. You will have a CT scan Monday for both your back and face (sinus fracture across your upper nose). First the back surgery, then, after you are stabilized, the sinus surgery.

It is windy and had snowed last night so some roads are drifted shut. Some friends called and said that they can't get here because the roads are too bad. Rick and Susie brought the boys and you and they were so excited. Now they feel much better with being able to see you for themselves.

On the way back to Auburn the white-outs were unreal. We saw a 16-20 car pile- up on I-69. It was so scary. Randy was going to bring me back but the county and state police closed most of the roads. There are accidents everywhere and no one could be out except for emergencies. So Rod brought Lacey, your dog, to our house and called you. She was so funny trying to find you on the phone. She slept with Rod and was so good.

Sunday, February 25, 1990

Rod and I took Lacey back to where I work. She ran all over while Rod dug my car out of the snow. The doors were even frozen shut. Lacey minds so well and looked so adorable sitting in the front seat with him.

It was a wonderful day for you.. It was nice to hear you laugh again. You had a string of visitors from 12:30 until 8:30. You were really tired.

Monday, February 26, 1990

Your CT scans are scheduled for today. You were so good this morning. You ate breakfast then I gave you a complete bath. You said that you felt 100% better and you wanted to go home.

About 3:00 p.m. a nurse said that you were craving water again. They had to do blood tests and found out that it was a chemical imbalance from the pituitary gland. They took you down for your scans and we will know the results tomorrow.

Tuesday, February 27, 1990

Your liquid restriction was lifted so now you can have all you want to drink. You are keeping the nurses busy day and night just giving you liquids. You had breakfast, a quick bath, a pain pill and Pepsi and are ready to go to physical therapy. They are just going to put you on a tilt table today to get you use to being up.

You are having more head (brain-you call it) pain now and your shoulder is bothering you a lot. I went on to work after your bath. You called me at work and said that the doctor had cancelled your back surgery. He said that your x-rays looked better and you could get by with a back brace for up to 12 weeks. Praise the Lord! Everyone is so excited.

Wednesday, February 28, 1990

8:00 a.m. The sun is shining and you are sleeping like a baby. It's so amazing to see you in a regular bed after 12 days in the roto rest. You are still craving liquids though, so we hope they get you started on the medications you need for the pituitary gland. You slept well except for waking up and needing water. A quick sponge bath, a Pepsi, and a pain pill and you are ready for physical therapy. They will be here at 10 a.m. to put you on a tilt table to get you use to being up. You did really well on the tilt table and will be going again this afternoon.

Thursday, March 1, 1990

In like a lamb, sunshine and 40 degrees today.

You hurt everywhere this morning—your head, shoulders, and especially your arm with the I.V. The nurse really upset you when she took blood. She did not wake you up first and then she tried both arms.

Physical therapy came in at 9 a.m. and you were so dizzy on the tilt table. The doctor came in and wants to wait a month or two before doing your facial/sinus surgery. He said it takes too much movement of your head so he wants to wait until you have healed.

The orthopedist wants you to get more therapy with sitting up and standing. He wants you to be able to walk before you can go home.

When I came back from supper time you were sitting up in a wheelchair (close to an hour.) Another doctor came to check your eyes. Our pastor came in and prayed for your sight healing.

Everyone is still praying for you and for a complete healing. You have touched so many people.

Friday, March 2, 1990

It has been two weeks today since the accident. You are so tired and said that your head and shoulder are hurting so bad. You are going to sleep after a little breakfast.

Saturday, March 3, 1990

You did so good today in physical therapy that your doctor released you. Your blood pressure is now stabilized when you are standing and moving.

It is up to the neurosurgeon as to where we go from here. You are thinking that it is home, but when he came in at 1:00 p.m. he said that your pituitary gland is still not working right. You were upset. You will have to have more blood tests and will have to be here until Monday to get the electrolytes in balance. Then, maybe, you can go home. He told you this is a life and death situation and if not exact you could go into toxic shock.

Sunday, March 4, 1990

I went back to church this morning to share with the congregation, who had at the time of the accident, made a circle in the church and prayed, visualizing as if your hospital bed was in the center of the church. I was able to share that we have yet another miracle—she will be coming home tomorrow!

Monday, March 5, 1990

Going home! After 18 prayer-filled days, Robin will be returning home with special instructions. She has a back brace, a nasal spray to stimulate her pituitary gland and strict orders not to be out on icy roads.

Robins View

I WAS THE DRIVER of the car, critical with barely a chance for survival—my head was crushed and my spinal cord was ready to sever. The Rescue Team was about to do their job to perfection. To them, it was saving a life, "my life." To me it was something I would learn about after coming out of a moderate coma one week later.

My mom kept a journal for me during the worst days telling what the doctors said and did, what I said and did, and things that my family was doing. She also kept a list of caring people who came to the hospital, called and were praying.

After seeing and sharing all the miracles with others, it's time for me to relive that day. I know God blocks the accident out to protect us, but I feel I missed the start of a true story that, when shared with others, could give hope and let people know miracles do happen.

From the moment that ice covered tree limb fell—until the Rescue Team got to me—God was with us all that day, giving them the knowledge and skills to get me out of the car and to the hospital alive and quickly. If not for them, the times I'd had with my family and husband would have been the last times shared.

We take a lot for granted in life. The Police, Fire Department, EMS, and the Rescue Team—knowing if we ever need them, they will be there. When it is your life they are saving, you realize God has picked a very special group to help Him with this task.

Trees really can fall; trees really can do a lot of damage. But thanks to God and the special people He has chosen, we can survive. We can show others our way of survival and maybe save another life somewhere.

Everyone was allowed to come in to see me that first night because I was not expected to live through the night. My best friends even came from Southern Indiana in the middle of the ice storm because they did not know if this was the last time they would see me alive. My head was as big as a basketball and my eyes were as big as grapefruits but no one thought to take a picture. I would only be able to envision this once I came out of my semi-coma. I was strapped to a bed because they did not know the extent of my injuries, but I somehow was able to get my feet out of the straps. This showed the doctors that I was not paralyzed, but I really could have been doing more damage at the same time. While I was in the coma, I would yell out "They killed my baby! They killed my baby!" over and over again. Everyone believed that I was talking about my white samoyed, Lacey, and my black lab, Ebby.

My family was told by the doctors that the first 72 hours would be the most critical. At that point, they could start assessing the damages. My back was broken and my skull was cracked open two layers from my eye clear to the back of my neck. All of my facial bones were crushed and my once perfect teeth were now chipped and the nerves were damaged. I also had a broken neck and a broken collar bone. My pituitary gland had also shut down. I had lost vision and was seeing double.

The doctors said that the cracks in my head were a good thing because it kept the pressure from building up and the swelling started to diminish after 72 hours. I was in and out of consciousness for the whole first week. It was not until I fully came out of the coma that the doctors were able to access the damages.

The first x-ray of my back showed that it was broken and that the spinal cord was only being held together by a thread. I could not be moved to get a better x-ray for fear that the thread would sever. By the second week, they were able to get a better x-ray before they took me to surgery to put a rod in my back. Miraculously the spinal cord had started to fuse back together and surgery was not required.

I would also be having fat tissue moved from different parts of my body up to my face to fill in the holes and the sinus cavities. I could only imagine how I would end up looking with fat from my thighs stuck to my face and forehead, not to mention what this would do to my self esteem.

The most extreme pain came from my collar bone being broken. It seemed funny that the least important thing could hurt the most.

The doctors started me on a nasal spray to help stimulate the pituitary gland. This took days for them to get the right dosage. In the mean time, I developed diabetes incipitus which caused a thirst which would not go away. I was constantly asking the nurses to give me more water. There was a bathroom with a toilet right in front of me. I knew there would be clean water in the toilet tank and I would bug everyone who came in to my room to get me some. I knew this because my brother had used the same trick when he was in the hospital to have brain surgery and was restricted on his water intake.

An ophthalmologist told me that I would regain my vision within a year. At least that is what I thought that I heard him say. What he actually said was that my vision may never come back. My peripheral vision was totally gone at this time, although the double vision that I was experiencing did clear up.

I had told God that I knew the colors of the sky and the grass and that if one person would come to know Him through all of this then it would be worth losing my eyesight. After spending many hours in the hospital with family and friends, we were able to see God working right in front of us. A man that is very dear and near to all of our hearts came to have a personal relationship with Christ.

I never wanted my mom to leave. I always made sure that she was close by. I was overwhelmed with the number of cards and flowers that everyone sent to let me know they were praying for me and thinking of me. My room looked more like a flower shop than a hospital room.

My mom would come in daily and read my new cards to me. She would sit by my bed and read the Bible to me and write in my journal. It was a comfort just to know that she was nearby.

After The Coma

A LIFELONG FRIEND OF mine, a nurse, came in and told me that she had scheduled herself to be in the operating room with me for my back surgery. My mom was so excited that a friend would be with me. As she was preparing me for surgery, the orthopedic surgeon came in and said that he had cancelled my back surgery because he felt that it would heal on its own with the help of a back brace. We were so excited about this news. I would get to go home earlier than expected. Then, the doctor came in and told us that he had cancelled my facial surgery because he was afraid of doing more damage to my broken neck. This was all part of God's perfect plan although we had no idea of what was ahead. We could only see what was in front of us; we could not see the big picture. Even so, God can and knew it would be amazing!

Going Home

IT HAD BEEN FIFTEEN days and I was getting very homesick. My brother even snuck my dog, Lacey, up to see me. I think Rod only brought her because she looked so cute sitting next to him in the Samari, but I was still excited to see her.

I had started physical therapy on the tilt table. I needed to regain my equilibrium. I had to learn to stand again after laying in bed all of those days. I just wanted to get the therapy done and over with so that I could get home. I almost fell down the stairs once because I was in such a rush to get things moving.

I thought that I would be able to go home on Friday, but my doctor said he wanted to keep me through the weekend to make sure they had the right dosage for my pituitary gland. Monday would definitely be the day I would be released. This news did not make my happy list. I desperately wanted to go home!

Monday arrived with a flurry of mixed emotions. I was most anxious to get home, but wondered if I would be able to get along without a push button for the nurse anytime I needed her. The drive home was scary as I was concerned about every bump we hit. The doctor said that a sudden jar to my back could still paralyze me.

I was back home after eighteen days in the hospital. My family and friends were not sure if I ever would return here. When I walked in the front door, everything was as I had left it. It was so good to be home! This was the start of an amazing path that the Lord had prepared just for me.

Every morning my mom would come over on her way to work to help me get settled for the day. She would crush my pills and put them in applesauce so I would not know they were there. My husband put our bed on the first floor of the house so I would not have to go up and down any stairs. My best friend's mom would then come over and spend the days with me. She would take me for walks. Many people came and visited me.

My first real outing was to go to church on Easter Sunday. I would get to see all of the people who had been praying that God would heal me. What a day of rejoicing this would be. It also helped that the dress that my mom had bought for me to wear that day was four sizes smaller than I had originally worn. This is one diet plan that I would not recommend for anyone.

We sang "Because He Lives I Can Face Tomorrow." I remember my mom looking over at me and smiling. We knew that it was because of God's grace that I had more tomorrows to face.

After church, the whole family went out for dinner and then back to the house for some much needed rest. It had been a long day, but a very happy day for my first day out.

A New Chapter In My Life

THE NEXT COUPLE OF months would be filled with doctor's appointments and trying to regain my strength. Today my brother called and wanted me to come and sit at the tanning salon so that our clients could see that I was okay. I had just drunk a gallon of milk and was throwing up. I told him that I would be there soon. It was nice to see all of the people again who had become part of my life the last couple of years. Life seemed to be getting back to normal.

It seemed each day brought different aches and pains and kept my mother busy phoning my doctor with inquiries. We were also concerned that I was not having my monthly period. Even so, the doctors had assured us that with a brain injury it could take years for that to start again. My husband and I were told at this point that we would never be able to have a family. We were newlyweds and this news was hard. I went to an OBGYN to see if my body would ever start working the right way again. The appointment was scheduled for the last week of July. I was very apprehensive about what I would be told. I knew that my back brace was getting tighter, but what if. What if I had just gained back the weight that I had lost-- what if the doctor was right and I never could have a baby. But what if in my semi coma when I was yelling "They killed my baby" there was really a baby growing inside of me. What if this was all part of God's perfect plan, for me to be pregnant before the accident.

I thought about all of this and could have been overcome with fear thinking about whether a baby would be alright after everything that I have been through. I knew that if the Lord was giving me a child, He was going to protect this precious child as He did me.

The day came for my appointment. I walked into the doctor's office, the same group of doctors that had delivered me. We were there just to see if my female organs would ever start to work again. I left my mom and my husband sitting in the waiting room when they called my name. We had no idea of what to expect. The doctor asked me a few questions and did not say much until he was done poking, measuring and listening to my midsection. What came next was truly one of God's miracles. As I sat up, the doctor announced that I was seven months pregnant and he had no reason to believe that this child would not be perfectly healthy.

As I made my way to the waiting room, the walk seemed like miles. Tears were streaming down my face and I could not wait to tell the news. "I AM SEVEN MONTHS PREGNANT!" I announced as I burst into the waiting room. My husband looked shocked and my mom burst into tears as she had just been telling everyone in the waiting room about the accident. Although excited and wanting to tell the whole world, we only told close friends over the weekend. My sister-in-law was going to make me an appointment with the OBGYN for Monday so that we could get an ultrasound done. The nurse practitioner called me at home thinking that I was lying in bed with tubes stuck all over and a blood pressure cuff on my arm and a big belly. She was very surprised when I walked in for my appointment. She was wrong about the tubes and blood pressure cuff but was right about the big belly.

I had worn a back brace for five months since I had been released from the hospital. I had to call my orthopedic surgeon to inform him that I was pregnant and ask him what I should do with the brace. He was not happy with me. I was told to wear the back brace for another month. What was I to do? I could not wear a brace with a growing belly. Once the brace was off, the baby shifted to a more comfortable position. I could once again breathe normally.

After a long day at the doctor where I had an ultrasound, we returned home. A good friend, who worked at the OBGYN office, called me to tell me that everything was great. She even knew the sex of the baby, but I would not allow her to tell me. Just knowing that everything was alright was enough. God's peace filled us! We would be expecting our little one the first week of October.

We had a short time to prepare for the arrival of our new little miracle. I was given many baby showers that helped get us ready for our baby. We spent time getting the bed ready as well as shopping for just the right equipment for out little baby. We attended Lamaze classes and I then decided that I did not want to go through with this. It was going to be way too painful. The doctor really wanted me to deliver naturally because of all that my body had already been through earlier that year.

The first week of October came and went—no baby. The second week of October came and went—again, no baby. The third week we were going to induce. On Wednesday, October 17, 1990, I went to the hospital to be induced. By Friday morning they were turning the medicines up every fifteen minutes. I was on my sixth bag of pitocin and was still not in labor. By Friday afternoon, I finally started to dilate. But the baby's heart rate started to change for the worse. The doctor decided that an emergency c-section would be for the best. At 4:24 p.m. the doctor announced that it must be a girl because the baby was stubborn and did not want to come out. But what a surprise, it was a boy! The doctor asked what his name would be and I announced Thomas Samuel. The doctor said that it sounded like he was going to be a doctor or a lawyer. At 21 inches long and 8 pounds 14 ounces, the nurse brought him over and let me touch his face. He looked just like my dad. They took him right away to the nursery. On the way, my family was able to see him. He was jaundiced, had low blood sugars and had a heart murmur.

After spending an hour in recovery, I returned to my room. That evening I was wheeled down to the nursery to hold my new son for the first time. It was amazing, even though I was scared. I couldn't believe that he was here. It was just a few months ago that we even found out about him. We had been through so much that it seemed we already had a special bond. Looking back, and seeing how the Lord protected him, I know that God has great plans for Tommy's future. He is in control.

The next couple of years we would be faced with many other trials. We had taken care of my dad, who had suffered with Emphysema, for four years. We cooked meals, cleaned his home and did his shopping. After he committed his life to Christ, my father passed away in April of 1999. He had moved to Denver to spend his last days with the rest of our family. I will never forget the night that we said our final goodbyes.

In February 2001, the next trial was something I never expected! Tommy was 10 years old and his father chose to leave our home and I became a single mom. It's as though we are watching a parade; we can only see what is in front of us, but God can see the end.

Photos

Scene Of Accident

Recuperating At Home

Robin

Grandpa and Tommy

Aren't I cute?

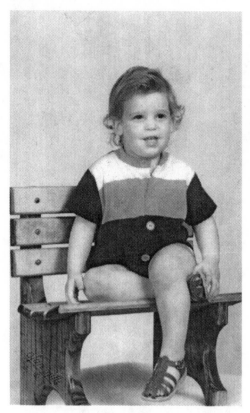

Tommy

My Classroom

Tommy #55

Playing the game

Robin And Tommy After
A Basketball Game

Summer 2004

TOMMY WOULD BE BUSY playing basketball this summer and attending many basketball camps. My mom, my step-father Sam and I repainted my kitchen, living room and hallway while getting plans ready to go see my brothers and their families in Denver, Colorado. Tommy and I would be experiencing a new adventure on this vacation as we took the train all the way out there. The 24 hour train trip would allow us to meet many new people with a wide variety of backgrounds. Years before we had made the same trip, but had taken a greyhound bus which was a real life experience for Tommy. The people we met were amazing.

The week before we left, I started to have swelling in my legs and hands and had so much pain in my body that I could hardly move. I went to my family doctor and he gave me several medications to help me get through until I could get to the internist in a neighboring town. It just so happened that my appointment was for the day that we were to leave on our vacation. I rescheduled the appointment for three weeks later when we would be home.

Spending time with my brothers and their families and seeing Tommy hanging out with his four cousins was priceless. I was in a lot of pain, but with the help of my medication, I was still able to enjoy the time away. My brothers and I were able to reminisce about my mothers past and how she had been able to overcome so much with the help of the Lord. We thought that she should someday write a book.

Tommy and I spent one day with my aunt and uncle at the place where my father had passed away years before. I felt as if I finally had closure on that part of my life because I was able to see where he spent his last days and was able to thank them for taking care of him.

Upon returning to Indiana, I met with an internist who scheduled two days worth of tests. The results showed a lump on my right lung, a mass in the middle of my chest possibly growing onto my heart and my blood work was all high with either cancer cells or an infection somewhere in my body. More tests would need to be done in order to determine what it was exactly. My doctor asked me if there was anything I needed to get me through the weekend. I told her that my dog really needed Ritalin but that I would be alright because I was confident that the Lord had this in His plan. The very next day, I was watching a show in which the mother had cancer. I couldn't help but wonder what it would be like if it were me. On Sunday, I made my way to the altar. Finding myself in tears, I told the Lord that I did not think that I could handle having cancer. I needed to be here to raise my son. My aunt and uncle were the elders who were praying with me and they anointed me with oil. Surrounded by family members, they prayed for the healing of my body.

Monday morning began with more tests. Tuesday we had to meet with my attorney to place my parents as power of attorney in case any emergent decisions needed to be made on my behalf. Tommy was only thirteen years old and he would not be able to make any medical decisions.

Wednesday arrived and I had to go to the hospital for outpatient surgery. As afraid as I was of the surgery and the results, I was even more concerned that someone I knew would see me at the hospital and start asking questions. School was to begin in two weeks and there was no time for doubting that I would be returning to my teaching position. The surgeon had to biopsy a part of my blood vessel to check for cancer cells in the blood. He would do this by cutting a slit up the hairline above my ear. My mom had worked with the nurses who assisted in the surgery and I knew the surgeon from the school where I taught. They gave me a local anesthetic and all I recall was talking the entire time.

Thursday, Randy called to ask if I was in the calm before the storm. My reply was that the storm was over and that tomorrow would be my "rainbow day." Friday morning we met with the doctor. Her first words as she walked into the room were that there was no cancer. My mom yelled, "Praise the Lord!" The doctor still wanted me to meet with the cardiologist to have a scope done to check the mass by my heart. Upon reviewing the test, the cardiologist did not feel as if it were necessary to perform the scope. He said that my heart had not changed in the four years since he had last seen me.

We went back to my moms to call my step-father, Sam. While we were there, my sister-in-law, Susie, called from Denver to check on how everything was. After telling her all the good news, she told us that Nick, her middle son, had just called, crying, saying he had signed his papers to go to Iraq. I left to come home to tell Tommy my good news and about Nick going to Iraq. My mom had given us money to go out to eat in order to celebrate. We decided to go tell my brother, Randy, and his wife. Coming around the curve on the way to his house, Tommy looked up and through his tears said, "Look mom, there is a double rainbow. It is God's promise that we are going to be okay."

August 2004

Starting school would be different this year. Not only would my health be in question, but my classroom would be under the direction of the church instead of the school and my classroom was moved downstairs. Now, I would have to go up and down flights of stairs every time I left my room. I received my class list which showed that my morning class would be 7 boys and 5 girls and that my afternoon class would have 5 boys and 1 girl. I had had the little girl the previous year and knew that not only could she hold her own against the five boys but she could also protect me.

I sat at my desk with just a few things on the wall and began praying. This is one thing that I would find myself doing more often this year, because I knew that God had a purpose in my being there this year and it was only by His grace that I was going to make it through another school year.

As school began, I would pray each day during our Bible lesson for each student by name. When it came time for the children to start praying, they also learned to pray for each student by name. Not only did this help them learn each others names, but also helped them to learn to care for one another.

Two weeks into the school year, I was once again back under the direction of the school. I felt like I was home again having the same principal and administrator.

I would schedule my weekly doctor's appointments after school so that I would not have to miss class time with my kids.

One Wednesday morning, on our way to chapel, the high school office helper gave me a note saying that I was to call my doctor as soon as I received the message. I sat my children down in chapel and had another teacher watch them while I went to make a phone call. On the way back from using the phone, I ran into the principal in the hallway. I had tears in my eyes and she knew that something was wrong. I told her that a MRI had shown spots on my brain and I was to go to the emergency room to meet a neurologist immediately. She would get someone to cover my class and I would wait for my mom and Sam to come and get me. By then, the principal had cancelled her appointments for the afternoon and went with us too. At this point, no one knew that I was losing my vision except for my mom and step dad. I was nervous about the principal finding out and it just so happened that when the neurologist asked me about my vision the principal's cell phone rang and she had to leave the room. I was safe for another day!

The doctor gave me a shot for my headache and told me to return in a week to have another MRI to see if the spots were moving or changing. The MRI showed that the spots were just scar tissue from my accident. A definite answer to prayer.

I would somehow survive Thanksgiving and Christmas but my yearly review was next. I knew that my students had learned what they needed to up to this point so I felt confident the day the principal came to sit in my room and observe me. Everything went just as I had planned and my review came back great. This was yet another obstacle that the Lord saw me through.

As the year progressed and my vision slowly deteriorated, I came up with ways to make the classroom run smoothly. I would call the students up to my desk and check their papers with them standing right beside me so that if I had questions, I could ask them. Each student was then to put their own papers in their mailboxes. If a student's grade was not a S+, I would put their name on a piece of paper and put it in the grade book. I would then go back later and find the boxes in the grade book to record their grades. Any teaching tools that I needed, I would get out the night before and make sure they were in the order that I would need them. I had taught this for so many years that the teaching part came natural and I did not struggle with it.

One Sunday in March, I woke up and could hardly see at all. I was sure that I was losing all of my sight then. I went to the altar and once again prayed for God's intervention. That week I would be going to a specialist that the neurosurgeon had recommended. I would have a MRI with pictures of my eyes done before I went. There was no vision in my left eye and only a dime size spot in my right eye that was a yellowish fog. The specialist said that there could be possible fluid behind my eyes and suggested a spinal tap be done. I came home to my doctor and he did a spinal tap and drained several vials of fluid off of my brain. The pressure then decreased. Then my vision was clear, but I had lost sight from the top and bottom of my right eye and my left eye was totally black. I was told that I had a false tumor in my brain that would keep producing this fluid. They could do one more spinal tap and eventually put in a shunt to drain the fluid.

It was March and I knew that I could make it just a few more months until school was out. Then they put a new little boy in my afternoon class. He could not speak English and while he had a lot to learn, he quickly found a warm place in my heart. If he left my classroom knowing that Jesus loved him, I knew that my job was complete. I only had a few more months to go and just because the green ink pad had help making marks all over my room and the crayons were being thrown up in the air making a rainbow of colors, I knew that the Lord was watching over us and that He was still in control.

I got so attached to my afternoon class of seven children. I loved just sitting on the floor and playing with them and watching them play with one another.

The last week of school was bittersweet. I was thrilled that I had made it through the year and that the students had learned what they were supposed to in order to move on to kindergarten. At the same time, I did not know where my future was going. After school had let out for the summer, I sat in my room and made sure everything was organized and in its place. I knew that I could not go back with the vision that I had, but I knew that the Lord had a plan and I would just hang on to that. I had to get everything in order just in case I had to turn my classroom over to someone else. A teacher friend would come and hang out in my classroom the way that he did all year and we would joke around. He would help keep my spirits high even though he did not know what was going on. He did not know that the Lord had sent him there for a reason until the end of the summer when he found out about my eyesight.

I would also have an eye appointment this week with a different eye specialist. After four hours of laughing and crying with us, she told us that the tumor was real and that the fluid would keep building up and eating away at the eye tissue until there was nothing left. The only thing that could slow down the progress of the tumor was to lose weight. She said that my vision could last for a day, a week, a month, or even up to six months.

I went to devotions at school the next morning and shared with everyone that my headaches were caused by built up fluid and that I needed to lose weight. I still did not say anything about my loss of vision because I truly believed that I would see again someday.

Telling Tommy

It was Sunday morning and after church. We would be going to my mom's house for steaks on the grill. Tommy sensed that there was something that we were not telling him. When we were done eating, we sat down with Tommy and my step dad told him about my vision. He rolled up a piece of paper to show Tommy exactly how much I could see. Tommy did not say a word. He just sat and listened.

That night when we got home, he sat on the couch with me and cried. We talked about how the Lord would take care of us and how He had gotten us through so much before and that He would not let us down now.

A Letter To My Mom

Mom, you are so amazing. I speak for everyone I know when I say you are an inspiration to us all. I know we do not see eye to eye all the time, but, in the midst of that, I still love you unbelievably much. I am so happy to see your willingness to serve God. Some people say you lose a sense when you go blind, but I think you gained one in your passion for Christ. This is a new thing that we are going through but with the love we have for each other and the love we have for God, we can get through it. When I look back, I realize that I should have made our time a full time of love, because time is short. But now I will make sure I do. I love you always more than anything.

Love, Tommy

Tommy's Viewpoint

FALL, 2005

It's a miracle I am even here because of the accident. My mom never told me about it until I was older and I realized I had a purpose from God. I hope that purpose is to play basketball. Basketball wasn't even my favorite sport until I was about in 4th grade when I realized I was alright at it. To have my mom at the games is just an amazing boost to me. There is no one like her although she isn't quite as crazy as Uncle Randy.

It was Mother's Day when I found out about my mom losing her sight. When my grandpa told me my heart sank into my stomach so far I just wanted to get away. My mom kept telling me it was okay and then a humbling feeling came to me just like God was crying with me. Through my mom's situation I have learned that though hard times come, you can still laugh and not just cry, you can still love God and not just turn your back on Him, and that you can come closer, not apart. There is not another person like my mom. She has raised me by herself pretty much and I hope she did a good job. Just kidding, she did.

I would like to write one more letter to my mom and then one to my friends and family.

Mom,

The Lord, I know, wants you to tell your story, and you're listening to His will. The love I have for you surpasses anything imaginable. Thank you so much for loving me even through the hardest of times. The Lord has many crowns awaiting you in Heaven. That day He says well done good and faithful servant, we all will rejoice because we know that we are with the ultimate love of our lives. I love you so much!

Love, Tommy

To my friends and family,

Cody, You've been my best friend since kindergarten. God wanted us to be that way I think. You make me laugh when I am down and are there with a shoulder when I am crying. Thank you so much man! You're awesome.

Bryan, My big Bro, wow man, one year went so fast but you took me in and showed me love. Thank you so much for that. So much sweat and tears we have shared on the court and off. We had some great times. Thank you so much. I love you man.

Uncle Randy, You are my dad figure. You can laugh with me and cry with me. You can be hard on me and be gentle too. Where would I be without you? I love you so much!

Coach Davis, Not only in basketball but away from it, you are a great influence. The first time I met you I was so intimidated, but then I realized how much you loved and care about me. Thank you so much for everything through this time.

Matt Franks, Another one of those dad figures. I love you so much man. You are always there to do anything with me. You are awesome!

Ashley, You give me that serious yet funny side of the situation. You understand that times are tough but yet you don't take it easy on me. Because of it, you toughen me up.

Tiffany, Sis, you are the one that can tell me anything and I can tell you anything and you care. You have loved me and my mom and it means a lot to us.

Paige, You pretty much rock! You are that person that when I walk through the hall I am just awed at the person you are. The love you have for Christ, and your passion for people is just amazing.

Thank you to everyone else I didn't mention. The Lord got me through a freak accident; He can get me through this stuff with people like all of you.

Telling the School

AFTER MANY NIGHTS OF prayer, the time had come to set up an appointment with the principal to talk about my teaching contract for the upcoming year. She just so happened to have a half hour time slot that afternoon. When we walked into her office, I instantly started crying, so my mom had to be the spokesperson. She listened intently as we told her that my eyesight had been deteriorating and I did not know if I would be able to continue teaching with the little eyesight that I still had left. The superintendent was out of town but she would get in touch with him and talk about what to do. She did not want me to clean out my room at this point. They handled the entire situation with love and grace.

On the way home, we stopped by Tommy's coach's house, with whom we have gotten really close to. He and his wife were out in the yard and we asked if we could talk with them for a few minutes. We told them the same thing we had just told the principal of the school. This helped them understand the many tears they had seen over the past several months. He had known that something was wrong because he had seen me all summer at the basketball games and knew that I was not myself. They were both very supportive and I knew that they would always be there for Tommy. The coach was like a father figure for Tommy so I knew that he would be a great help to Tommy as he learned to deal with the new challenges that lie ahead for him.

Now that the school knew, I was able to tell people that I would not be going back when they asked if I was ready for school to start. A teacher friend arrived back after the summer and was shocked that he had never suspected anything after hanging around me. He would call and check on me and hang out with Tommy. I would often ask him what would happen if the doctor was right and I did lose all of my sight. He always told me to trust in God because He is in control.

My "New Normal"

August 2005

After an intense evaluation, it was time to start learning to live life in my "new normal." Over the next couple of months, life would be filled with many emotions, frustrations, and even a few happy moments. Even though I had worked on preparing myself for this, I knew I could not make it through this without the Lord carrying me.

The day arrived when my trainer was coming to teach me how to live in a dark world. My family was all here to offer me support. A car drove by and everyone thought it was the trainer. We watched as the car turned around, but at the same time, the phone rang. It was the trainer saying he was not coming that day. I was relieved but disappointed at the same time. I really wanted to get started, but now I would have to wait until the following week. This was another lesson from God in patience.

The following week when the trainer arrived, we started by filling out some papers. He told us that 87% of everything you learn is through your eyesight; and we would be going through a grieving process as if someone close to us had actually died. My first lesson was on how to find things on the table. This way I would not look so dumb when I was at the table eating with other people. What I really wanted was to receive the "cane" so that other people would be made aware of my visual loss without my having to tell them. But this was not to be the day.

Many weeks passed before my trainer was able to come back. I strived to make things as normal as possible for my fourteen year old son during this time. I started to prepare him for his first year in high school, knowing that I would not be returning with him. These were the days that I did not allow myself to think about preparing lesson plans, rearranging my classroom, and getting excited about the upcoming school year. Instead, I focused on the joy of my life, Tommy. Tommy would be playing varsity basketball this year as a freshman and I needed to prepare myself that I would be at the games but would struggle to see him on the court. In the past, it was always so fun to watch him because not only was he a good player, he would laugh and always encourage his fellow teammates. I had been the cheerleading coach so I was able to cheer extra loud. He was given the leadership award in junior high, but I knew that going from junior high to high school varsity would be a challenge. I knew that with all these challenges in his life that God was preparing him for something big. This is what made me want to go on.

The first week of school, my mom and my friends kept me busy every day. One friend even took me to the library and set up weekly delivery of books on tape. Even so, I would look forward to the minute that Tommy would get home. We would just sit and talk about how great his day was and how much he loved high school. Everything seemed so right during those moments. I loved being a mom!

When the trainer came back, we talked about the "cane" that I referred to as a stick, but he kept correcting me that it was a cane. We talked a lot about my expectations as well as what he expected from me. My homework was to name my cane and do wrist exercises to strengthen my wrist because even though the cane only weighed 10 ounces, after a day of training, it would feel as if it weighed 10 pounds. To help take my mind off of the reason I was exercising my wrists, I would go into the back yard and throw the ball over and over again to our 70 pound, yellow lab, Porscha. I had her trained to just lay the ball in my lap each time she brought it back to me. This was also a time when I would listen to my books on tape.

The next time the trainer came, he taught me how to instruct other people how to walk with me. We went through the house visualizing where everything was, but after living in my home for the past thirteen years, I could picture everything in its place. We had already spent the summer preparing the house to make it easier to get around as I continued to lose my sight. One such way we prepared was by exchanging bedrooms with my son. Tommy, being 6 foot 4 inches, had already outgrown his twin bed and could easily fit the bigger bed by lying diagonally. The smaller room would now become mine, thus giving me a smaller space in which to get lost. After repainting and rearranging the furniture, everything seemed to be ready for us to face the challenges that lie ahead.

The next few months with the trainer brought even more frustrations—cooking! Before I could pass cooking, I had to pass the skills of boiling, frying, baking, grilling and the use of a knife. I had to listen for the sounds of boiling water and timers going off while hoping that I had set them all correctly. How was I supposed to know when my meat was done frying in a pan? My sense of smell served me well. I told several friends that I was going to write a book titled "Cooking in the Dark with Hamburger Helper." A food drive, given by the children from the school where I had taught, brought in 96 boxes of Hamburger Helper. Since the recipes were similar on all of the boxes, I was able to be creative in my cooking; hoping Tommy would eat without asking too many questions.

Each week I had to prepare something for the trainer. He made me eat what I cooked, but he never would. I made goulash, potato soup, mini pineapple upside down cakes, chicken, macaroni and cheese and steak fajitas. I accidentally cut the trainer's finger with the new knives that he had brought. I had to do an extra lesson on frying because I had burned my wrist while frying pork chops. The only problem that I still struggle with is filling the sink too full with water. When he told me that I had passed cooking, I said "Great, let's order a pizza."

Chara Arrives

THE TRAINER ARRIVED BRIGHT and early today. Our lessons were becoming more intense as we strived to make the most of each day. We talked about the expectations and the laws of the cane. We discussed how the cane was a symbol that most people respected and how it was never to be used as a weapon. As the trainer went to his car to get the cane, I was in tears with mixed emotions. On one hand, I was ready for the cane because it would be a symbol that I was visually impaired and deter questions. I would no longer feel rude when I ran into people I knew but could not recognize them. I felt safer with the cane. On the other hand, the cane made everything seem so final.

I named my cane CHARA which means joy. I wanted it to always remind me that no matter what life holds, I have the joy of the Lord. A teacher once told me that my middle name should be Joy because I was always so happy. I was not sure at this time that I could live up to this name, but the joy of the Lord is my strength.

One training session I told my trainer that it was a little easier to use the cane around people that I did not know. I was still apprehensive in using the cane in places where people knew me. It was fine just tucked into the front pouch of my backpack. While I was at school just the day before, I took the cane out of my backpack, ready to open, but stopped. I could not get myself to open the cane in the school, so I slowly tucked it back, safe and sound, into its pocket. Guess what? The trainer took me straight to the school to practice using my cane. We worked on stairs and finding corners. The kindergarteners and first graders were on their way to recess so we took a little break for a few quick hugs and hellos to former students. We explained to the students that the trainer was teaching me new things just like I had taught them new things. We also ran into Tommy who was showing our pastor around the school for Pastor Appreciation Week. I got an extra special hug from my son that day. God knew just what I needed on a day that I was so unsure about.

As I learned to use the cane over the next few weeks, I experienced walking in all types of weather. My trainer said this was luck to be able to do this first hand, but I knew that it was all in God's plan for me—not luck. I even had the joy of walking in the rain. It was only because of my new designer umbrella that made me look cute that I even went along with this. I knew that we would be walking on the busiest street in my hometown. This was a very humbling day as I walked downtown in the rain, with my cane, with my umbrella and a man who looked like Santa Claus behind me. As we went into winter, I would always wait for the phone call in the morning telling me that the weather was too bad to be out walking with Chara, a name that my trainer still has not gotten used to. With winter came six inches of snow and I had the joy to walk in the snow with Chara. The trainer said he knew that I would just call someone to come get me instead of ever using this training but also said that I did very well.

Today was to be a testing day. My trainer would give me a destination and that was where I was to meet him. I would be on my own for the very first time. He would be watching me from somewhere, but I would not know where. This was two days before Thanksgiving. I was fearful that I would not find my way and that I would not be home in time for Thanksgiving. When my trainer arrived that morning, I told him that I had put out an APB and an Amber alert on myself knowing that I would be lost. He told me to meet him at the school which was eight blocks away from my home and said that he would meet me there. I actually made it to my destination and I knew that he was indeed there when I heard his voice. After walking a few blocks, he twirled me around eight times and said find your way home. After doing all the steps that he had taught me, I realized that I was hitting the gutter on the side of someone's home. Hoping that they would hear my knocks and come to help would certainly be the best scenario, but I knew this was something I needed to do on my own. I just needed to concentrate. After saying a little prayer, I listened for traffic and found my way home.

Crossing at streetlights was next on the agenda for mobility. After being in the local newspaper with different articles, I was sure that the people in my hometown would be helping me out. People would honk their horns and yell "Hi, Robin" and I would always want to say, "Can you give me a ride home?" But I persevered, and put to use the skills the trainer was trying to teach me.

Learning To Read Again

OVER MY MANY YEARS of teaching, I had taught my students that letters lived in houses. I was now learning that letters also live in boxes. I would learn this by using a muffin tin and sugar packets. In Braille, each letter of the alphabet is made up of a series of bumps. I had to learn that each box has six cells and certain letters lived in certain cells. My fingers had to be my eyes as I learned which bumps belonged to which letter.

"Many Blessings"

As my life turned into the darkness, and I was guided by His light, not a moment went by that His presence was not known to me. Not only did He give me the strength to learn my new normal, but I was blessed with so much more. The principal had put the devastating news about my loss of vision in the last newsletter of the summer that she sent out to all of the school families. I received many calls from caring people wanting to know how they could help. The principal had a meeting and those who attended gave many suggestions and ideas of things that they would like to do for Tommy and I. One idea was to have a food drive that coincided with a school fund raiser already in progress. Each grade was given a specific type of non perishable food item to bring in. The students really got into this and went above and beyond what we ever expected. One grade even had a contest between the different classes to see which class could bring in the most boxes of cereal. The food drive lasted for three weeks and a total of 988 items were brought in. It was a real challenge to find room for that many cans of soup, vegetables and fruit, juice, boxes of cereal, boxed meals, laundry detergent and softeners, paper towels, toilet paper, toothpaste, shampoos and bath soap. We could have become a distributor for the local grocery store. Our shelves looked better than a convenience store. One of my friends joked that on Halloween night when he came trick or treating that he would like toothpaste, pop tarts, and a can of soup.

Another idea was to have meals brought in once a week since I would be volunteering at the school every Wednesday and would have my trainer here twice a week. They would also get three teams of three people and clean my house every other week. This was a tremendous help!

One other suggestion was to have a spaghetti dinner and a bake sale. This too was bigger than expected and they served almost 500 people. Even people that knew me when I was two came out to support me and Tommy. The bake sale sold out by noon. My mom is still trying to get them to do another bake sale because she did not get to buy anything the first time because they sold out so quickly.

One friend even came in and cleaned out and organized

my cupboards so that I could more easily find things when I needed them.

I found myself going out to eat a lot with caring friends and one day even went out for breakfast twice. Many friends even called me to see if I needed anything from the grocery store or would just stop by to visit and keep me company. These were the times I was most grateful that my friends were helping me keep my house clean.

The talk among my friends was to have my house made over on a television show. One of the ladies who organized the spaghetti dinner woke up one Saturday morning and the Lord told her to have a community project. The plans were then moved in this direction. In one week's time, she had an article in the local paper and many volunteers. The Lord's hand was definitely overseeing this project.

When I first started losing my sight, I saw a movie about a blind girl who always seemed the happiest when she was soaking in a bath full of bubbles. I did not even have a bathtub in which to soak. We only had a small shower. Because of caring friends, we got a new shower and bathtub put in right after Christmas. When my friend told me there was going to be even more work done on the house, I was amazed. I know God is huge, but it was more than I could have ever imagined. When the garage came tumbling down, and the walls to a whole new addition on the house went up, it was evident that the Lord was working through the community to show his love to me and Tommy. With the new addition, I would have room to put all of my new equipment from the League for the Blind and Lions Club. These are things that are making life easier and more independent for me. This room would also make more space for Tommy and his friends.

Hope

I LOOK FORWARD TO the day when the Lord will return, but until then I know that I will never truly be in the darkness because I will be guided by His light. I know that I will see again someday and if not here on earth, then can you imagine, the first thing I will see is Jesus' face.

A Word of Thanks

To my family: This has been an incredible journey that we have been on. We have had many tests and trials along the way and this seems to be the hardest. God's love shining through all of you has given me strength. Your understanding and support have been a testimony to your faithfulness to God. I thank God for you everyday! I love you all!

To my friends: You are amazing. Your love and kindness has carried me through the worst times. Tom, Diane, Robin, Power Plus Girls, Hope Group, my school and church families, and so many others who have helped in so many ways, I love you all. Someone always seems to call, come over or do a good deed just when I need encouragement.

To Ron Brunger: For the vision of this amazing cover. Thanks Uncle Ron.

To Jeana: Where do I start? Yeah, where do I start? Would a simple "thanks" do it? Love you!

To Sue and Julia: You're incredible! The Lord has many crowns waiting for you.

To Debbie: You helped me survive the training to learn how to live in my "new normal." You learned as much as I did from the trainer, and I think that he liked you better. Thanks so much for all of the laughs, even when my mom made us work. I am truly blessed that the Lord has let our paths cross through our children.

To Pamela: Thanks for the vision for writing my story. I am grateful that the Lord brought us together. Your love and support has carried me through. Your willingness to help me with everything has been a true blessing. Thanks so much for all you have done!

To Don, Jess, and David: Thanks for the shoulders to cry on. You were the ones that just let me cry and didn't ask questions during the worst times.

To My Tommy: You have learned character, integrity, and strength through tragedy. You have grown into a young man who has never taken his eyes off of the Lord. He has given you great athletic ability with your mom as your biggest fan. Always remember God has given you this gift! I am looking forward to your future. My love for you is unconditional and forever!

Printed in the United States
94547LV00001B/223-321/A